# Artisan Bread

# Cookbook

*The Ultimate Handcrafted*

*Illustrated Bread Cookbook with*

*No-Fuss Recipes for Perfect*

*Homemade Breads*

**GORDON RIPERT**

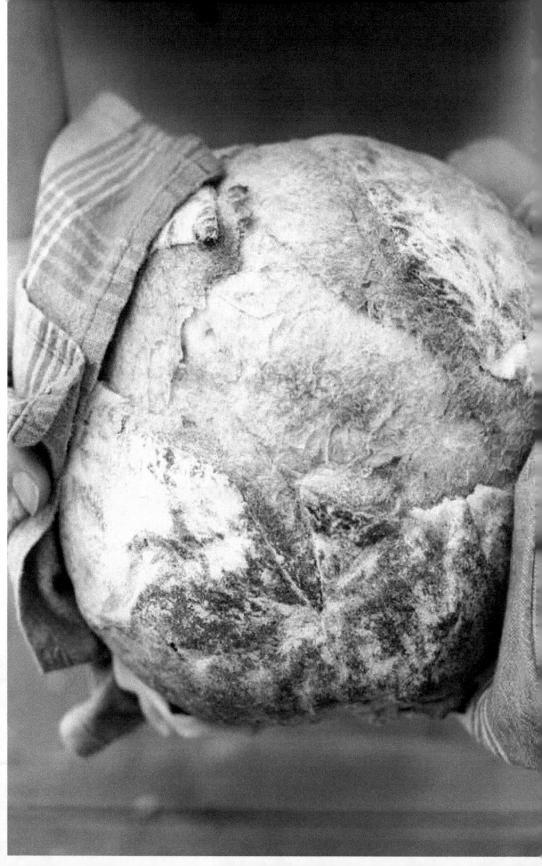

# Table of Contents

**INTRODUCTION** ..................................................... **8**

WHY SHOULD YOU USE A BREAD MACHINE? ...............................10

BREADMAKING TAKES LESS WORK ................................10

THEY'RE EASY TO USE...................................................11

BREADMAKERS USE LESS ENERGY THAN A TRADITIONAL OVEN ...................11

BREAD MACHINES ARE VERSATILE...................................12

BREAD MACHINES MAKE BETTER BREAD ..........................12

CHOOSING A BREAD MACHINE.......................................13

HOW MUCH SPACE WILL IT TAKE UP?..............................13

HOW MANY TYPES OF BREAD CAN I MAKE? ......................13

WHAT ARE THE OTHER FEATURES AVAILABLE?....................14

HOW MUCH DO I WANT TO SPEND?.................................15

MOST POPULAR BRANDS...............................................15

BREAD MACHINE UPKEEP AND CLEANING ........................16

OILING THE KNEADING SHAFT......................................16

CLEANING...................................................................17

**CHAPTER 1: BREAD MACHINE CYCLES/SETTINGS**...................**18**

FEATURES: CYCLES AND SETTINGS .................................18

BASIC.........................................................................19

SWEET BREAD ............................................................19

FRUIT AND NUT ..........................................................20

VARIETY .....................................................................20

DOUGH ......................................................................21

WHOLE WHEAT ...........................................................22

FRENCH BREAD ...........................................................22

ONE HOUR CYCLE.........................................................23

BAKE ONLY .................................................................23

PROGRAM ...................................................................24

JAM ..........................................................................24

DELAY FEATURE ..........................................................25

PREHEAT ....................................................................25

CRUST CONTROL..........................................................26

**CHAPTER 2: TROUBLESHOOTING** ....................................**28**

MISTAKES WHEN MAKING BREAD ..................................28

No rise ................................................................................................ 28

Coarse texture ................................................................................. 29

Crust too light ................................................................................. 29

Too much rise ................................................................................... 29

Dense and short ............................................................................... 30

Crust too thick ................................................................................. 30

Sunken top ........................................................................................ 31

Mushroom top .................................................................................. 31

Gummy ............................................................................................... 32

Crust too dark ................................................................................... 32

Pro Tips to Make Perfect Bread ................................................. 32

Measurements Make a Difference ............................................. 33

Don't use liquid measures for dry ingredients, and vice versa ........ 33

Don't skip the salt! .......................................................................... 33

Get a conversion chart, app, or magnet for the fridge ................... 34

Quality Matters .............................................................................. 34

Recipes All Have a Reason ........................................................... 35

Check Your Settings ....................................................................... 36

Buttermilk Basics ........................................................................... 37

Try Something New ........................................................................ 38

Consistency Checks ........................................................................ 38

**CHAPTER 3: CLASSIC BREAD** ....................................................... **40**

Almond Flour Bread ...................................................................... 40

Coconut Flour Bread ..................................................................... 43

Cloud Bread Loaf ............................................................................ 45

Sandwich Buns ................................................................................ 47

French Bread .................................................................................... 49

**CHAPTER 4: WHOLE-WHEAT BREAD** ........................................ **51**

Butter Honey Wheat Bread ......................................................... 51

Buttermilk Wheat Bread .............................................................. 53

Cracked Wheat Bread .................................................................... 55

Honey Whole Wheat Bread .......................................................... 57

Maple Whole Wheat Bread .......................................................... 59

**CHAPTER 5: NUT AND SEED BREAD** ......................................... **61**

Lemon Poppy Seed Bread ............................................................ 61

Macadamia Nut Bread ................................................................... 64

Super Seed Bread ............................................................................ 66

Cranberry Walnut Bread ............................................................... 68

APPLE WALNUT BREAD................................................................71

**CHAPTER 6: ITALIAN & FRENCH BREAD** ................................**73**

ITALIAN SEMOLINA BREAD .......................................................73
DELICIOUS ITALIAN BREAD........................................................76
ORIGINAL ITALIAN HERB BREAD ..............................................78
ITALIAN ONION BREAD .............................................................80
CRISPY FRENCH BREAD DELIGHT .............................................82

**CHAPTER 7: SPECIAL BREAD**.................................................**84**

KETO BREAKFAST BREAD ..........................................................84
CHIA SEED BREAD ....................................................................86
KETO FLAX BREAD ...................................................................88
SPECIAL KETO BREAD ..............................................................90
KETO EASY BREAD ...................................................................92
LOW CARB BREAD....................................................................94
SPLENDID LOW-CARB BREAD ..................................................96
BREAD DE SOUL .......................................................................98
SANDWICH FLATBREAD...........................................................101
KETO SANDWICH BREAD .........................................................103

**CHAPTER 8: FRUITY BREAD AND CAKE**...............................**105**

BANANA BREAD ......................................................................105
BLUEBERRY BREAD..................................................................107
APPLE WITH PUMPKIN BREAD..................................................109

**CHAPTER 9: ROLLS AND PIZZA** ............................................**111**

CAULIFLOWER PIZZA CRUST ....................................................111
MOZZARELLA PIZZA CRUST......................................................114
ZUCCHINI PIZZA CRUST ...........................................................116
FAT HEAD PIZZA DOUGH - EGG & GLUTEN-FREE .....................118
KETO PIZZA POCKETS ..............................................................121

**CONCLUSION**........................................................................**123**

# Introduction

A bread machine is basically a small, electric oven. It fits one large bread tin with a special axle connected to the electric motor. A metal paddle connects to the axle, and this is what kneads the dough. If you were making the bread in a mixer, you would probably use a dough hook, and in some instructions, you'll see the bread machine's kneading part referred as a hook or "blades."

The first thing you do is take out the tin and add the bread dough you made in Step 1. Bread machines can make any kind of bread, whether it's made from normal white flour, whole wheat, etc. Pop this tin unto the axle and program by selecting the type of bread, which includes options like basic, whole-wheat, multigrain, and so on. There are even cycles specifically for sweetbreads; bread with nuts, seeds, and raisins; gluten-free; and bagels. Many models also let you cook jam.

You'll probably see a "dough" mode option, too. You would use that one for pizza. The machine doesn't actually cook anything; it just kneads, and then you take out the pizza dough and bake it in your normal oven. If you aren't making pizza dough, the next selections you'll make are the loaf size and crust type. Once those are chosen, press the "timer" button. Based on your other selections, a time will show up, and all you have to do is push "start."

A bread machine is both a "kneader" and a small oven. Using a metal paddle and heating element, the bread machine kneads and bakes for a certain amount of time, based on what kind of bread you're making. All brands and models will include basic cycles like white, wheat, and multigrain.

After kneading and before the machine begins baking, many people will remove the dough so they can take out the kneading paddles since they often make an indent in the finished bread. The paddles should simply pop out, or you can buy a special hook that makes the removal easier. Now you can return the bread to the machine. The lid is closed during the baking process. If it's a glass lid, you can actually see what's going on. You'll hear the paddle spinning on the motor, kneading the dough. It lies still for the rising stage and then starts again for more kneading if necessary. The motor is also off for the proving stage. Next, the heating element switches on, and steam rises from the exhaust vent as the bread bakes. The whole process usually takes a few hours.

## Why Should You Use A Bread Machine?

You know how a bread machine works, but why should you think about getting one? There are five main reasons why this device should be a part of your kitchen assembly: less work for you, ease of use, less energy wastage, versatility, and a better final product:

## Breadmaking takes less work

There's a lot of work involved in making bread by hand. When you use a machine, that machine does a lot of the busy stuff for you. You just add your dough, and the breadmaker starts doing its thing, giving you time to do other chores or sit back and relax. As a note, not all breadmakers are completely automatic, so if you want this benefit, you'll probably have to pay a bit more money. It's worth it for a lot of people, though. Some Panasonics even have "yeast pockets," which add yeast at the perfect time after the paddles knead the dough, so you don't have to do that part, either!

## They're easy to use

The first question most people ask when investigating a new kitchen device is: Is it easy to use? Bread machines are indeed easy to use. If you can use a crockpot or a microwave, you can use a bread machine. Cycles and other settings like loaf size and color are always clearly marked, and once you do a quick read of your instruction manual, you'll be ready to go. Recipes written for bread makers are also very clear about what settings you need to select, so as long as you follow them, your bread will turn out the way you want.

## Breadmakers use less energy than a traditional oven

Ovens require a lot of electricity, and when you're making bread, that long bake time can make an impact on your energy bill. They also lose a lot of energy because the oven is much larger than necessary for one loaf of bread. Breadmakers are smaller and, therefore, more efficient. There's also a lot of variation from oven to oven in terms of heat, while bread machines are more consistent across the board. This consistency translates into better bread no matter what recipe you're using.

A bread machine is a great appliance because they're easy to use, they are more energy-efficient than a regular oven, they let you make a wide variety of recipes, and they often make better bread because of the machine's precision.

## Bread machines are versatile

You can make more than just regular sandwich bread with a bread machine. As you'll see in the recipe section of this book, you can make buns, breadsticks, and even cakes. Many breadmakers even have a "Jam" setting, so you've got the makings of an afternoon tea snack in just one device. The bread machine can also be used just for kneading, which is very useful when it comes to making pizza dough. While you can't cook the dough in the bread machine, you can have the machine do the hard part.

## Bread machines make better bread

If you've struggled with making the perfect loaf in the past, a bread machine could change all that. Specific cycles for different types of bread ensure you're also choosing the right to knead and bake time, so there's much less guesswork. The best machines calculate all the other variables for you, too, like how much yeast to add and when to add other ingredients like nuts, and so on. You can really tell the difference in texture and taste when every step is precisely carried out by a breadmaker.

# Choosing a Bread Machine

While Panasonic is the original and best-known brand for bread machines, there are others well worth looking into. When you're pursuing bread machine options, you want to ask yourself the following questions:

## How much space will it take up?

Bread machines aren't compact kitchen gadgets. They take up a fair amount of counter space and storage space when they aren't in use. Machines are typically measured by how big of a loaf they can make. A larger machine can bake 2-pound loaves. The actual machine will weigh a lot more; for a 2-pound loaf machine, expect a total weight of around 10 pounds. Think about how much space you have in the kitchen and on your counter before choosing a machine.

## How many types of bread can I make?

What kind of bread you can prepare with a bread machine comes down to how many programs or cycles it has. Some have as few as six cycles, but most have 12-14. There are even bread machines that only knead the dough, so just make sure the one you're looking at does indeed bake, as well. The most common programs on bread machines include Basic, French, Gluten-Free, Sweet, Quick (no yeast), Express (which uses a quick-rising yeast), Dough (for pizza crust), Cake, and Jam. If you're really into experimenting with bread, there's even a 25-program bread machine from Aicok with more unusual types like Rice Bread, Low-Sugar, Italian Cake, and settings that let you roast nuts and make yogurt. For most people, a 12 or 14-setting bread machine is the right fit.

## What are the other features available?

Besides bread programs, it's a good idea to look at other features that come on the bread machine, such as the ability to delay baking or a heated lid for more even browning on top. One of the best features of Panasonic breadmakers are the models with yeast dispensers, which add yeast to dough at exactly the right time. For now, it appears that Panasonic is the only brand with this feature. Other brands, however, sometimes have fruit/nut dispensers that are great for making raisin bread and more. The Breadman 2-Pound Professional Bread Maker is one such model. As for a bread machine with both dispensers, there's the Panasonic SD-YR2500, which is in the upper range in terms of price.

When considering a bread machine, think about factors like its size, how many kinds of bread you can make, extra features like yeast dispensers, and how much it costs.

## How much do I want to spend?

Speaking of price, how much you want to spend should also be a consideration when shopping for bread machines. There's a wide range starting at around $50 all the way into the $300's. With bread machines, a lower price does not necessarily mean an inferior product. It usually means fewer programs and smaller size. For the average home baker, one of these more affordable machines makes sense. If you are more experienced with recipes and want to make as many types of bread as possible, be prepared to spend a bit more money. Always check out what other customers are saying and how the company handles complaints.

## Most Popular Brands

The following brands appeared in Spruce Eat's list of best bread machines for 2018:

- Oster

- Panasonic

- Zojirushi

- Breadman

- Hamilton Beach

- T-Fal ActiBread

- Cuisinart

## Bread Machine Upkeep and Cleaning

Like with any kitchen gadget, taking care of your bread machine is important for its longevity and for safety. These appliances can last for years when they're well-cared for, so here's what to do:

## Oiling the Kneading Shaft

The kneading blades are the crucial part of the machine that kneads the dough. You'll see the blade shaft when you turn over the pan, as well as a little wing nut and clip. Every six months or so, it's a good idea to oil this shaft to keep it working smoothly. It will ensure your bread machine lasts for years to come. However, you can't use just any oil. You want to use 3-in-1 oil or sewing machine oil. Other types of oil can cause rust and other damage, while oils like WD-40 actually become toxic when exposed to heat.

You want to apply oil only on the outside shaft on the underside of the bread pan. It should not go inside the bread pan at all. Use just 1-2 drops and oil around the metal ring on the underside. Turn the wing nut to work the oil in. Wash your hands well after handling the oil. In terms of maintenance, oiling the kneading shaft twice a year is really all you need to do.

## Cleaning

What supplies do you need when cleaning your machine? Not much. A clean rag, a non-abrasive dish soap, warm water, and a brush, like one would use for basting. You won't be using all of these things for every cleaning job, so read carefully. Before beginning to clean, be sure the bread machine is unplugged and completely cool. Here's how to clean the three main parts of the machine and three types of messes.

# Chapter 1: Bread Machine Cycles/Settings

## Features: Cycles and Settings

The owner's manual will familiarize you with the different parts of the machine, some basic DIY steps for removal and replacement of the bread pan, and the correct order to add the ingredients in the pan. In addition, the manufacturer will list out the features, also known as the cycles of the machine. The purpose of this list is to inform you of the types of bread that your machine can make and the exact time needed to make a loaf on each of these settings. The manual will also use a chart to tell you how long each cycle lasts. Note that the amount of time for each cycle depends on each machine brand. The following cycles are the most common in all machines:

## Basic

This is also known as Basic Bread, Basic Wheat, Basic Mode, White or Standard bread. This setting is most commonly used for all purposes. The cycle lasts for up to three to four hours, based on your machine, and is used for whole-wheat or whole-grain bread and white bread that are made up of more than 50 percent bread flour. You can also use this cycle instead of a French Bread cycle or if your machine doesn't have a French bread cycle. In this Basic cycle, there is sometimes the option for "Quick" or "Rapid." Or your machine can have the options in a separate cycle. On many of the newer models, there's an inbuilt alert that goes off when you need to add any extra ingredients, such as raisins or nuts.

## Sweet Bread

This cycle makes doughs with higher sugar and fat content to rise slower than usual. This Sweet Bread cycle has a longer rise time and a reduced baking temperature, just about 250°F. This is because the crust of the sweet bread will brown faster. The inbuilt indicator in this cycle beeps when it's time to add the extra ingredients to the mix, such as chopped glacéed fruit or nuts. Also, many sweetbreads are mixed, shaped in the Dough cycle, and baked in the home oven.

## Fruit and Nut

This cycle is also known as the Raisin Mode or Mix Bread cycle. This setting is used when nuts, chocolate chips, seeds, or dried fruits are added to the dough. With this method, the extra ingredients are not overmixed or completely blended during the extreme speed of the blade action during the kneading phase of the cycle. Many of the newer models have an audible alert inbuilt as part of the Basic and Whole Wheat cycles, rather than built-in a separate cycle. When the alert sounds, it is time to open the lid and add the extras. But if your machine doesn't have this cycle, you can use the Basic cycle for bread with extra ingredients. When I want to try a different taste or color for my bread, I add extras like onions and nuts at the start of the cycle. That way, it is completely pulverized and disintegrates into dough by the time the kneading action is complete.

## Variety

This feature was common on the older models. This cycle runs for about the same amount of time that the Basic cycle runs. It has an indicator beep and also displays the signal to "shape" at the second rise, so the dough can be removed, filled and shaped by hand, and then returned to the baking pan for the final rise and baking. This cycle can also be used for a monkey bread or cinnamon swirl.

If your machine does not have this feature, you can get it by programming the Basic cycle, pause to interrupt the cycle after the second rise, remove the dough and shape, then return it to the baking pan and press Start to resume cycle and bake the bread.

## Dough

This setting is also known as the Rise or Manual cycle. It is perfect for when you want to mix and rise a dough in the machine, then remove the dough, shape it by hand, and bake it in your oven. The setting with the shortest dough cycle is Toastmaster at 1 hour and 3 minutes with 1 hour, 30 minutes as the average, while the Panasonic brand is the longest cycle at 2 hours, 30 minutes (including Preheat). Doughs that are prepared on this cycle are meant to be shaped into traditional loaves or into special shapes like egg twists, cloverleaf dinner rolls, pizza, breadsticks, croissants, or bagels, and baked in the oven. You can adjust your favorite recipes for this cycle, and using quantities that will fit in your machine. When the alert beeps, remove the dough and follow the instructions on the menu to start shaping. In this cycle, there's sometimes a provision for the further options of Basic Dough or Quick Dough.

## Whole Wheat

Also known as the Basic Wheat mode Whole Grain, it allows heavy whole grain flours to have a long kneading time and a rising time slightly longer than the Basic cycle rising time, producing a loaf that is lighter and higher. It is especially recommended for 100 percent whole-grain or whole wheat bread, and for bread that are made of specialty flours like barley or spelt. You can also have the choice of Basic or Quick setting within the cycle. On many of the newer models, their indicator alerts have been inbuilt such that it beeps to indicate when you should add any extra ingredients like raisins or nuts during the cycle. Some of the models that have the preheat option at the beginning of their cycle usually preheat during the Whole Wheat cycle.

## French Bread

A Crisp, European, or Homemade setting is usually available for the same purpose. This cycle is generally well-liked and well-received by users of bread machine baking. This setting is suitable for crusty country bread with zero sugar and fat because they require a longer length of time to rise, and it also affords the yeast a long while to do its work. Older bread machines often have this cycle, and it usually lasts for seven hours, which would be perfect for a traditional baker from France. It is also good for sourdough bread that contains yeast. The baking temperature of this cycle is about 325°F. The bread baked using this cycle is usually crisp with a soft inner crumb.

## One Hour Cycle

The One Hour cycle is another type of shortened cycle that produces bread within one hour. The One Hour cycle eliminates more than one rise and is even more rapid than Quick Yeast Bread. Similar to the Quick Yeast Bread, the One Hour Cycle requires the use of instant or quick-rise yeast. Your owner's manual will provide information on how to regulate the yeast in a recipe for this cycle. I have personally noticed a decrease in taste and quality in bread made with this cycle, so I don't endorse using it. The One Hour cycle can be replaced with the Quick Yeast cycle when making gluten-free yeast bread.

## Bake Only

In newer models of Bread Machine, a Bake Only cycle is sometimes programmed so that a dough prepared on the Dough cycle can be shaped into desired forms and then returned to the machine for baking. It can also be used for a cinnamon swirl bread, a hand-mixed dough, a commercial dough, or in the event that you initially planned to bake your dough in the normal oven but changed your mind. When a cycle ends and your dough is not properly done, the Bake Only cycle is invaluable, and you can program it to bake in increments for up to two hours. If you are doing different types of baking, this cycle works best.

## Program

Certain machines have a function that allows a manual change of the cycle times to your preference while being able to increase kneading, rising, or baking time as you need it. You can also program in the times for each of your recipes such that when you use a particular recipe, you don't need to program the time anymore, although this feature is only used by people who have become expert bakers and are proficient with the basic cycles.

## Jam

Some newer machines have a feature where you can add small fresh fruit jams, with or without pectin, and at the same time make fruit butter and chutneys. Make jam only in a machine designed for that purpose to prevent spills or leakage.

## Delay Feature

This is a common and well-liked feature because you can program the machine at night and have fresh bread in the morning or meet fresh bread when you get home from work. There are some recipes that are not suitable for this cycle, such as recipes that include fresh ingredients like milk, cheese, eggs, fresh vegetables, and bacon, as they can become harmful at room temperature and turn sour or even result in food poisoning. The bread that requires dry milk and powdered eggs are suitable for use with the Delay Timer. For optimum results while using the Delay Timer, make sure the yeast doesn't come in contact with the salt (because it would restrain its rising power)nor come in contact with any liquid (it would activate it before the mixing began) when the ingredients are together in the bread pan. Pour the liquid ingredients before any other; the salt should come after, then the dry ingredients and the yeast should come at the end. Or switch the order around to suit your machine requirements. Many bread machine manuals insist on this precaution for all recipes, but it is only needed when using the Delay Timer.

## Preheat

Some bread machines have a Preheat or Rest period setting, which helps to keep ingredients put in the machine at uniform temperature by the time mixing starts, just like how we used to warm flour on the oven door to encourage good rising and allow the yeast to perform at optimum capacity. This phase ranges from 15 to 30 minutes, and the machine will be quiet during this phase since the blade is inactive. Some of the more complex machines allow you to ignore this feature, but others don't. It is inbuilt in every baking cycle on some machines, while others like Breadman machines only have it on their Whole Wheat cycle. Some people believe this feature produces better bread and like this feature, and some don't like it because it increases the time of the whole process.

## Crust Control

This is a setting that gives you the option of light, medium, or dark crust in addition to being able to choose the cycle for your loaf. It does this by slightly altering the baking temperature or timing slightly. That way, you get to decide the finished look of your loaf. The crust setting also influences how well done a loaf is because it changes the baking time and temperature. For basic and whole-grain bread, I normally use the medium or normal crust setting, and I regularly check the loaf to make sure the bread is thoroughly baked.

If the crust on your bread comes out too light and the loaf is not properly baked, for another time, choose the dark crust setting and if the crust comes out too dark and the bread is overdone, choose light for the crust setting. Some people may like their whole wheat bread with light crust while some prefer dark crusts on their French bread, but I normally set the crust on dark for my artisan and country bread, while light for sweetbread, because they brown more quickly as a result of the higher sugar content. Note that certain ingredients in the loaf have a direct effect on how the crusts brown, so it's best to experiment with the crust setting.

# Chapter 2: Troubleshooting

## Mistakes When Making Bread

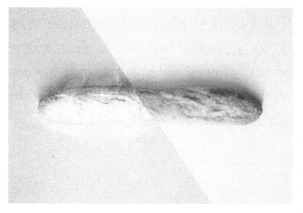

Your success in making bread in a bread machine can be affected by many different factors, which means a recipe that turns out a wonderful loaf one day may not produce the same loaf a week later. The bread will probably still be delicious, but it might not look exactly right. Here are some common bread-making issues:

## No rise

- Yeast is old or stored improperly
- Measurement of ingredients is wrong
- Flour has a low gluten content
- Too little yeast
- The temperature of ingredients is too high

- The temperature of ingredients is too low

- Too much salt

- Too much or too little sugar

## Coarse texture

- Too much liquid

- Too little salt

- Too much yeast

- Fruit or vegetables too moist

- Weather too warm or humid

## Crust too light

- The crust setting is too light

- Too little sugar

- Recipe size is too large for the bucket

## Too much rise

- Too much yeast

- Too little salt

- Water temperature is incorrect

- The bucket is too small for the recipe size

## Dense and short

- Bread doesn't rise (see No rise)

- Ingredients were added in the wrong order

- The dough is too dry; there is too much flour (not enough liquid)

- The size of the bucket is too large for the recipe

- Too much whole-grain flour or whole grains

- Too much dried fruit

- Too many other ingredients such as vegetables, nuts, or coconut

## Crust too thick

- Bread is left in the machine after the baking cycle is complete

- Flour has too little gluten

- Bread doesn't rise high enough (see No rise)

## Sunken top

- The bread machine was opened during the baking cycle

- Humid or warm weather

- Too much liquid in the recipe

- Liquid ingredients are too warm

- Ingredients were measured wrong or out of proportion

- The bread rose too far, disrupting the baking and cooling cycles

- Too much yeast

## Mushroom top

- Too much yeast

- Too much water

- Ingredients are out of proportion or measured wrong

- Too much sugar or too many sweet ingredients

- The size of the bucket is too small for the recipe

## Gummy

- Too much sugar

- Too much liquid or too many wet ingredients

- The temperature outside the machine is too cold

- The thermostat in the machine is defective

## Crust too dark

- The crust setting is too dark

- Bread is left in the machine after the baking cycle is complete

- Too much sugar

## Pro Tips to Make Perfect Bread

Whether you're just baking bread for the first time or you just want to bake better goodies, this section will give you all kinds of helpful insight to ensure that you make the most of your baking. From important elements to quick fixes and even simple basics, you'll find it all here.

## Measurements Make a Difference

When it comes to baking, measurements are not merely a suggestion. Rather, they are a science. You have to be very careful about measuring out your ingredients. For starters, make sure that you go to a kitchen store or shop online to supply your kitchen with actual measuring tools. Make sure that you have liquid and dry measuring tools in various sizes.

The biggest mistakes that you want to avoid include:

## Don't use liquid measures for dry ingredients, and vice versa

Tbsp and Tsp are interchangeable for liquid and dry. Cups, however, are not. If you need two cups of water, it needs to be two liquid cups. Don't believe there's a difference? Use a dry cup measure and fill it with water. Then, pour it into your liquid measuring cup. You'll quickly see that the measurement is less than exact.

## Don't skip the salt!

Unless you are specifically altering a recipe for sodium content (in which case you should find a low or no-sodium version), salt is an ingredient for a reason, and you cannot leave it out. Even if it seems like it wouldn't make a difference, it could ruin a recipe.

## Get a conversion chart, app, or magnet for the fridge

There are plenty of kitchen conversion guides out there that you can keep on hand. That way, if you need to convert measurements or make substitutions, you know exactly how to do it. You'll find all of your cooking and baking to be more enjoyable when you have conversions and substitutions at hand at all times.

If you're still in the beginner stages, you'll want to stick to the book as best as you can until you get the hang of things. Once you branch out and start to experiment, you can toss these rules out the window (except the liquid/dry measure one). The deliciousness of baking is in the details, and you cannot afford to make simple mistakes when it comes to measurements. There is a reason for the recipe, so if you want to get the best result, follow the instructions to the letter.

## Quality Matters

When you are baking anything, the quality of the ingredients that you use will make a difference. It isn't to say that the store brand flour isn't as good as the name brand because it very well might be. However, you should be careful in choosing a higher-quality ingredient in order to get better results. If you have the choice, go to a baker's supply or a local bakery outlet to buy the good stuff at better prices. If not, make sure that you get to know your basic ingredients and which ones are best.

The more familiar you get with your own baking abilities and preferences, the more you will be able to decide for yourself where quality matters most. Until then, keep these tips in mind. Also, remember that higher protein content counts with your flour if you're baking bread. More protein means stronger gluten, which makes better bread. Cake flour has a softer texture and lower protein count, which makes it ideal for baking cakes and other desserts.

## Recipes All Have a Reason

A lot of people prefer just to "throw in" the ingredients or measure hastily, which is fine if you're an expert or you're baking something that you've made 100 times before. If, however, you are trying to replicate something out of a recipe book, you need to follow the recipe. Even a single missed ingredient or mismeasurement can turn your bread into something completely different than what you wanted.

It's not like you are going to ruin everything by taking on baking with reckless abandon. If you're new at the bread machine game, though, you should get used to what you're doing before you throw caution to the wind and throw the recipe aside once you remind yourself of the baking temperature.

Even if you concoct your own recipes over time, you'll want to write down at least a rough estimate of what the measurement is. It's hard to share recipes that don't have finite measurements. While you might know exactly how much a "little" salt is, other people can't measure that accurately. Cooking takes skill, but baking is a science, and it should be treated as such.

## Check Your Settings

Again, the process is important. In that, you should also be sure that you check the settings of your bread machine before you start any new baking program. Even if you think you left it on the right setting or programmed the right feature, you need to double-check every time. There is nothing worse than waiting an entire hour to realize that you've been using the wrong setting. At that point, your recipe will most likely be ruined.

For beginners, the pre-programmed settings should be perfect, for the most part. There are a lot more options for those who are more experienced with bread machines like the bread machine, and everyone will get there eventually. When in doubt, use the programs and features on the machine, and let it make the hard decisions for you. You'll get great results, and if the program isn't exactly right, you'll at least have a starting point to begin making adjustments.

## Buttermilk Basics

Some people might not even understand exactly what buttermilk is. You don't have to be embarrassed; a lot of people don't know what this weird baking ingredient is for. Buttermilk, traditionally, was what was left after the cream was churned into butter. Most of the buttermilk that you find on the shelves today is cultured or made.

Buttermilk is used because it adds a slight tang to baked goods. It also increases the rise of the bread or pastry by reacting with the baking soda in the recipe. Buttermilk is in a lot of bread and dessert recipes. However, not everyone just happens to keep buttermilk around. If you aren't in the habit of keeping it around, or if you decide to bake something at the last minute, there is a solution. You can take a liquid measuring cup (one cup is fine). In a measuring cup, add a tbsp of lemon juice in the. Next, add milk up to half cup mark. Allow it to sit for a little bit, and voila, you have homemade buttermilk.

## Try Something New

Experimenting is good. If you're a novice at baking bread or just starting to learn your bread machine, you might not want to stray too far from the traditional. However, if you are willing to make mistakes for the sake of success, experiment away! As you get more experienced in baking bread with your bread machine, you will be more comfortable in changing things up and seeing what all you can make on your own.

You can try ingredient substitutions, such as the common use of applesauce as a sweetener in baked goods. You can add ingredients to existing recipes, change baking times and temperatures, and even try and create your own great recipes using your bread machine.

## Consistency Checks

The big difference with baking bread, compared to other cooking, is that you need to keep an eye on the consistency. While the good old "lightly brown" rule does stand in most cases, the consistency can be very different in a bread machine like the bread machine. Make sure that you capitalize on that "pause" feature and give yourself the chance to check in on your baked goods from time to time to ensure that they turn out their best.

You don't need to interrupt your baking processes too often. One should be enough. When you're making bread, it's a great idea to pause to remove the paddle, and at the same time, check on the bread and see how it's coming along. Not only does that allow you to ensure that the consistency is right, but it also allows you to get that paddle out before it's baked into the loaf and becomes a chore to remove.

# Chapter 3: Classic Bread

## Almond Flour Bread

**Preparation Time**: 10 minutes

**Cooking Time**: 10 minutes

**Servings**: 10

**Ingredients**:

- 4 egg whites

- 2 egg yolks

- 2 cup almond flour

- 1/4 cup butter, melted

- 2 tbsp psyllium husk powder

- 1 1/2 tbsp baking powder

- 1/2 tsp xanthan gum

- Salt

- 1/2 cup + 2 tbsp warm water

- 2 1/4 tsp yeast

**Directions:**

1. Use a small mixing bowl to combine all of the dry ingredients, except for the yeast.

2. In the bread machine pan, add all the wet ingredients.

3. Add all of your dry ingredients, from the small mixing bowl, in the bread machine pan. Top with the yeast.

4. Set the bread machine to the basic bread setting.

5. When the bread is done, remove the bread machine pan from the bread machine.

6. Let cool slightly before transferring to a cooling rack.

7. The bread can be stored for up to 4 days on the counter and up to 3 months in the freezer.

**Nutrition**:

- Calories: 110

- Carbohydrates: 2.4 g

- Protein: 4 g

- Fat: 10 g

# Coconut Flour Bread

**Preparation Time**: 10 minutes

**Cooking Time**: 15 minutes

**Servings**: 12

**Ingredients**:

- 6 eggs

- 1/2 cup coconut flour

- 2 tbsp psyllium husk

- 1/4 cup olive oil

- 1 1/2 tsp salt

- 1 tbsp xanthan gum

- 1 tbsp baking powder

- 2 1/4 tsp yeast

**Directions**:

1. Use a small mixing bowl to combine all of the dry, except for the yeast.

2. In the bread machine pan add all the wet ingredients.

3. Add all of your dry ingredients, from the small mixing bowl, in the bread machine pan. Top with the yeast.

4. Set the bread machine to the basic bread setting.

5. When the bread is done, remove the bread machine pan from the bread machine.

6. Let cool slightly before transferring to a cooling rack.

7. The bread can be stored for up to 4 days on the counter and up to 3 months in the freezer.

**Nutrition**:

- Calories: 174

- Carbohydrates: 4 g

- Protein: 7 g

- Fat: 15 g

# Cloud Bread Loaf

**Preparation Time**: 10 minutes

**Cooking Time**: 15 minutes

**Servings**: 10

**Ingredients**:

- 6 egg whites
- 6 egg yolks
- 1/2 cup whey protein powder, unflavored
- 1/2 tsp cream of tartar
- 6 oz sour cream
- 1/2 tsp baking powder
- 1/4 tsp garlic powder
- 1/4 tsp onion powder
- 1/4 tsp salt

**Directions**:

1. Using a hand mixer beat egg whites and cream of tartar together until you have stiff peaks forming. Set aside.

2. Combine all other ingredients into another bowl and mix.

3. Fold the mixtures together, a little at a time.

4. Pour mixture into your bread machine pan.

5. Set the bread machine to quick bread.

6. When the bread is done, remove the bread machine pan from the bread machine.

7. Let cool slightly before transferring to a cooling rack.

8. The bread can be stored for up to 3 days on the counter.

**Nutrition**:

- Calories: 90

- Carbohydrates: 2 g

- Protein: 6 g

- Fat: 7 g

# Sandwich Buns

**Preparation Time**: 10 minutes

**Cooking Time**: 25 minutes

**Servings**: 8

**Ingredients**:

- 4 eggs

- 2 ½ oz almond flour

- 1 tbsp coconut flour

- 1 oz psyllium

- 1 ½ cup eggplant, finely grated, juices drained

- 3 tbsp sesame seeds

- 1 ½ tsp baking powder

- Salt to taste

**Directions**:

1. Whisk eggs until foamy, and then add grated eggplant.

2. In a separate bowl, mix all dry ingredients.

3. Add them to the egg mixture. Mix well.

4. Line a baking sheet with parchment paper and shape the buns with your hands.

5. Bake at 374F for 20 to 25 minutes.

## **Nutrition**:

- Calories: 99

- Fat: 6 g

- Carb: 10 g

- Protein: 5.3 g

# French Bread

**Preparation Time**: 2 hours 30 minutes

**Cooking Time**: 30 minutes

**Servings**: 14

**Ingredients**:

- 1 1/3 cup warm water

- 1 ½ tbsp olive oil

- 1 ½ tsp salt

- 2 tbsp sugar

- 4 cup all-purpose flour; or bread flour

- 2 tsp yeast

**Directions**:

1. Put the warm water in your bread machine first.

2. Next, put in the olive oil, then the salt, and finally the sugar. Make sure to follow that exact order. Then put in the flour, make sure to cover the liquid ingredients.

3. In the center of the flour make a small indentation, make sure the indentation doesn't go down far enough to touch the liquid. Put the yeast in the indentation.

4. Set the bread machine to the French Bread Cycle.

5. After 5 minutes of kneading, check on the dough. If the dough is stiff and dry, add ½ - 1 tbsp of water until the dough becomes a softball.

6. If the dough is too wet, add 1 tbsp of flour until the right consistency is reached. Let the bread cool for 10 minutes before slicing.

**Nutrition**:

- Calories: 121
- Fiber: 1.1 g
- Fat: 1.9 g
- Carbs: 2.9 g
- Protein: 3.9 g.

# Chapter 4: Whole-Wheat Bread

## Butter Honey Wheat Bread

**Preparation Time**: 3 hours 5 minutes

**Cooking Time**: 15 minutes

**Servings**: 12

**Ingredients**:

- 1 cup water

- 2 tbsp margarine

- 2 tbsp honey

- 2 cup bread flour

- 1/2 cup whole wheat flour

- 1/3 cup dry milk powder

- 1 tsp salt

- 1 (25 oz) package active dry yeast

**Directions**:

1. Follow the order of putting the ingredients into the bread machine recommended by the manufacturer.

2. Run the bread machine for a large loaf (1-1/2 lb) on the Wheat setting.

**Nutrition**:

- Calories: 57

- Total Carbohydrate: 8.5 g

- Cholesterol: < 1 mg

- Total Fat: 1.9 g

- Protein: 2.1 g

- Sodium: 234 mg

# Buttermilk Wheat Bread

**Preparation Time**: 6 hours 8 minutes

**Cooking Time**: 15 minutes

**Servings**: 12

**Ingredients**:

- 1 1/2 cup buttermilk

- 1 1/2 tbsp butter, melted

- 2 tbsp white sugar

- 3/4 tsp salt

- 3 cup all-purpose flour

- 1/3 cup whole wheat flour

- 1 1/2 tsp active dry yeast

**Directions**:

1. In the bread machine pan, measure all ingredients in the order the manufacturer recommended. Set the machine to the Basic White Bread setting.

2. Start the machine.

3. After a few minutes, add more buttermilk if the ingredients do not form a ball, or if it is too loose, put a handful of flour.

**Nutrition**:

- Calories: 160

- Total Carbohydrate: 30 g

- Cholesterol: 5 mg

- Total Fat: 2.1 g

- Protein: 4.9 g

- Sodium: 189 mg

# Cracked Wheat Bread

**Preparation Time**: 3 hours 5 minutes

**Cooking Time**: 15 minutes

**Servings**: 12

**Ingredients**:

- 1 1/4 cup water
- 2 tbsp margarine, softened
- 2 tbsp dry milk powder
- 2 tbsp brown sugar
- 1 1/4 tsp salt
- 3 cup bread flour
- 1/3 cup whole wheat flour
- 1/4 cup cracked wheat
- 1 1/4 tsp active dry yeast

**Directions**:

1. In the bread machine pan, measure all of the ingredients in the order the manufacturer suggested.

2. Choose regular/light cycle; then start.

**Nutrition**:

- Calories: 50

- Total Carbohydrate: 7.3 g

- Cholesterol: < 1 mg

- Total Fat: 1.9 g

- Protein: 1.4 g

- Sodium: 271 mg

- Sodium: 189 mg

# Honey Whole Wheat Bread

**Preparation Time**: 3 hours 5 minutes

**Cooking Time**: 15 minutes

**Servings**: 10

**Ingredients**:

- 1 1/8 cup warm water (110F/45C)

- 3 tbsp honey

- 1/3 tsp salt

- 1 1/2 cup whole wheat flour

- 1 1/2 cup bread flour

- 2 tbsp vegetable oil

- 1 1/2 tsp active dry yeast

**Directions**:

1. Put the ingredients into the bread machine following the order recommended by the manufacturer.

2. Choose the Wheat Bread cycle and the setting for Light Color on the machine.

**Nutrition**:

- Calories: 180

- Total Carbohydrate: 33.4 g

- Cholesterol: 0 mg

- Total Fat: 3.5 g

- Protein: 5.2 g

- Sodium: 79 mg

# Maple Whole Wheat Bread

**Preparation Time**: 3 hours 5 minutes

**Cooking Time**: 15 minutes

**Servings**: 10

**Ingredients**:

- 2 1/2 cup whole wheat flour

- 1/2 cup bread flour

- 1/3 tsp salt

- 1 1/4 cup water

- 4 tbsp maple syrup

- 2 tbsp olive oil

- 1 1/2 tsp active dry yeast

**Directions**:

1. Put the ingredients into the bread machine pan following the order suggested by the manufacturer.

2. Choose the Wheat Bread cycle on the machine and press the Start button.

**Nutrition**:

- Calories: 144

- Total Carbohydrate: 26.9 g

- Cholesterol: 0 mg

- Total Fat: 2.8 g

- Protein: 4.3 g

- Sodium: 67 mg

# Chapter 5: Nut and Seed Bread

## Lemon Poppy Seed Bread

**Preparation Time**: 10 minutes

**Cooking Time**: 4 hours

**Servings**: 6

**Ingredients**:

- 3 eggs, pasteurized

- 1 ½ tbsp butter, grass-fed, unsalted, melted

- 1 ½ tbsp lemon juice

- 1 lemon, zested

- 1 ½ cup / 150 grams almond flour

- ¼ cup / 50 grams erythritol sweetener

- ¼ tsp baking powder

- 1 tbsp poppy seeds

**Directions:**

1. Gather all the ingredients for the bread and plug in the bread machine having the capacity of 1 pound of bread recipe.

2. Take a large bowl, crack eggs in it and then beat in butter, lemon juice, and lemon zest until combined.

3. Take a separate large bowl, add flour in it and then stir in sweetener, baking powder, and poppy seeds until mixed.

4. Add egg mixture into the bread bucket, top with flour mixture, shut the lid, select the "basic/white" cycle or "low-carb" setting and then press the up/down arrow button to adjust baking time according to your bread machine; it will take 3 to 4 hours.

5. Then press the crust button to select light crust if available, and press the "start/stop" button to switch on the bread machine.

6. When the bread machine beeps, open the lid, then take out the bread basket and lift out the bread.

7. Let bread cool on a wire rack for 1 hour, then cut it into six slices and serve.

**Nutrition**:

- Calories: 201
- Fat: 17.5 g
- Carbohydrates:    5.8 g
- Protein: 8.2 g

# Macadamia Nut Bread

**Preparation Time**: 10 minutes

**Cooking Time**: 4 hours

**Servings**: 8

**Ingredients**:

- 1 cup / 135 grams macadamia nuts

- 5 eggs, pasteurized

- ½ tsp apple cider vinegar

- ¼ cup / 30 grams coconut flour

- ½ tsp baking soda

**Directions**:

1. Gather all the ingredients for the bread and plug in the bread machine having the capacity of 1 pound of bread recipe.

2. Place nuts in a blender, pulse for 2 to 3 minutes until mixture reaches a consistency of butter, and then blend in eggs and vinegar until smooth.

3. Stir in flour and baking soda until well mixed.

4. Add the batter into the bread bucket, shut the lid, select the "basic/white" cycle or "low-carb" setting and then press the up/down arrow button to

adjust baking time according to your bread machine; it will take 3 to 4 hours.

5. Then press the crust button to select light crust if available, and press the "start/stop" button to switch on the bread machine.

6. When the bread machine beeps, open the lid, then take out the bread basket and lift out the bread.

7. Let bread cool on a wire rack for 1 hour, then cut it into eight slices and serve.

**Nutrition**:

- Calories: 155

- Fat: 14.3 g

- Carbohydrates:    3.9 g

- Protein: 5.6 g

# Super Seed Bread

**Preparation Time**: 5 minutes

**Cooking Time**: 22 min

Servings: 7

**Ingredients**:

- 2/3 cup entire psyllium husk
- 1/4 cup chia seeds
- 1/4 cup pumpkin seeds
- 1/4 cup hemp or sunflower seeds
- 1tsp ground sesame seeds or ground flaxseeds 1 tsp preparing powder
- 1/4 tsp salt
- 1 tsp coconut oil
- 1 1/4 cup fluid egg
- 1/2 cup unsweetened almond milk

**Directions**:

1. In a huge blending bowl, include every single dry fixing and blend well. You can make your own ground sesame seeds by mixing them until they're a fine powder.

2. Melt the coconut oil in the microwave (around 30 seconds), add it to the dry blend and mix well. At that point include 1/4 cup fluid egg whites and 1/2 cup unsweetened almond milk. Blend well and let the blend represent 10-15 minutes while you preheat your stove to 325° F.

3. Wet some material paper under warm water and shake it off, at that point press it into a 9" x 5" bread tin. Include your blend and press it into the edges of the tin. You can likewise add some additional seeds to the highest point of the blend here. Trim the abundance material paper and put it in the stove for 70 minutes.

4. Slice the whole portion and let cool on a drying rack. This bread can empty if not cut at the earliest opportunity and left to cool on a rack.

**Nutrition**:

- Cal: 70

- Carbs: 4g

- Net Carbs: 2.5 g

- Fiber: 4.5 g

- Fat: 8 g

- Protein: 8g

- Sugars: 3 g

# Cranberry Walnut Bread

**Preparation Time**: 10 minutes

**Cooking Time**: 3 hours

**Servings**: 14 slices

**Ingredients**:

- ¼ cup water

- 1 egg

- 3 tbsp honey

- 1½ tsp butter, softened

- 3¼ cup bread flour

- 1 cup milk

- 1 tsp salt

- ¼ tsp baking soda

- 1 tsp ground cinnamon

- 2½ tsp active dry yeast

- ¾ cup dried cranberries

- ½ cup chopped walnuts

- 1 tbsp white vinegar

- ½ tsp sugar

**Directions**:

1. Add each ingredient except the berries and nuts to the bread machine in the order and at the temperature recommended by your bread machine manufacturer.

2. Close the lid, select the basic bread, medium crust setting on your bread machine, and press start.

3. Add the cranberries and walnuts around 5 minutes before the kneading cycle has finished

4. When the bread machine has finished baking, remove the bread and put it on a cooling rack.

**Nutrition**:

- Carbs: 24 g

- Fat: 2 g

- Protein: 4 g

- Calories: 130

# Apple Walnut Bread

**Preparation Time**: 5 minutes

**Cooking Time**: 2 hours 30 minutes

**Servings**: 14 slices

**Ingredients**:

- ¾ cup unsweetened applesauce
- 4 cup apple juice
- 1 tsp salt
- 3 tbsp butter
- 1 large egg
- 4 cup bread flour
- ¼ cup brown sugar, packed
- 1¼ tsp cinnamon
- ½ tsp baking soda
- 2 tsp active dry yeast
- ½ cup chopped walnuts
- ½ cup chopped dried cranberries

**Directions**:

1. Add each ingredient to the bread machine in the order and at the temperature recommended by your bread machine manufacturer.

2. Close the lid, select the basic bread, medium crust setting on your bread machine, and press start.

3. When the bread machine has finished baking, remove the bread and put it on a cooling rack.

**Nutrition**:

- Carbs: 15 g

- Fat: 8 g

- Protein: 3 g

- Calories: 130

# Chapter 6: Italian & French Bread

## Italian Semolina Bread

**Preparation Time**: 10 minutes

**Cooking Time**: 3 hours

**Servings**: 6

**Ingredients**:

- 1 cup (220 ml) water

- 1 tsp salt

- 2 ½ tbsp butter

- 2 ½ tsp sugar

- 2 ¼ cup wheat flour

- 1/3 cup semolina

- 1 ½ tsp dry yeast

**Directions**:

1. The bread maker should be in the SANDWICH mode (on mine, this is 11 mode, 3 hours). With this program, you can mix, raise, and bake light bread with a crisp crust. The duration of the program is 3 hours.

2. In my bread maker, there is no preheating. The program starts immediately with kneading. If your bread machine has a program for Italian bread, then most likely, it will work as well. In some bread machines, a similar program is called SANDWICH. If there is neither, use the closest description.

**Nutrition**:

- Calories: 302

- Total Fat: 10.7 g

- Saturated Fat: 5.2 g

- Cholesterol: 13 g

- Sodium: 763 mg

- Total Carbohydrate: 45.9 g

- Dietary Fiber: 1.2 g

- Total Sugars: 1.8 g

- Protein: 6.2 g

# Delicious Italian Bread

**Preparation Time**: 10 minutes

**Cooking Time**: 2-3 hours

**Servings**: 8

**Ingredients**:

- ⅔ cup water at 80F

- 1 tbsp olive oil

- 1 tbsp sugar

- ¾ tsp salt

- 2 cup white bread flour

- 1 tsp instant yeast

**Directions**:

1. Add all of the ingredients to your bread machine, carefully following the instructions of the manufacturer.

2. Set the program of your bread machine to Basic/White Bread and set crust type to Medium.

3. Press START.

4. Wait until the cycle completes.

5. Once the loaf is ready, take the bucket out and let the loaf cool for 5 minutes.

6. Gently shake the bucket to remove the loaf.

7. Transfer to a cooling rack, slice, and serve.

**Nutrition**:

- Total Carbs: 26 g

- Fiber: 1 g

- Protein: 3 g

- Fat: 2 g

- Calories: 136

# Original Italian Herb Bread

**Preparation Time**: 10 minutes

**Cooking Time**: 3 ½ hours

**Servings**: 10

**Ingredients**:

- 1 cup water at 80F

- ½ cup olive brine

- 1 ½ tbsp butter

- 3 tbsp sugar

- 2 tsp salt

- 5⅓ cup flour

- 2 tsp bread machine yeast

- 20 olives, black/green

- 1 ½ tsp Italian herbs

**Directions**:

1. Cut olives into slices.

2. Add all of the ingredients to your bread machine (except olives), carefully following the instructions of the manufacturer.

3. Set the program of your bread machine to French Bread and set crust type to Medium.

4. Press START.

5. Once the maker beeps, add olives.

6. Wait until the cycle completes.

7. Once the loaf is ready, take the bucket out and let the loaf cool for 5 minutes.

8. Gently shake the bucket to remove the loaf.

9. Transfer to a cooling rack, slice, and serve.

**Nutrition**:

- Total Carbs: 71 g

- Fiber: 1 g

- Protein: 10 g

- Fat: 7 g

- Calories: 386

# Italian Onion Bread

**Preparation Time**: 10 minutes

**Cooking Time**: 3 - 4 hours

**Servings**: 8

**Ingredients**:

- 1 cup warm milk, at room temperature
- 1 large whole egg
- 2 tbsp butter, soft
- ¼ cup dried onion, minced
- 1½ tsp salt
- 2 tbsp dried parsley flakes
- 1 tsp dried oregano
- 3½ cup bread flour
- 2 tsp dry yeast

**Directions**:

1. Add all of the ingredients to your bread machine, carefully following the instructions of the manufacturer.

2. Set the program of your bread machine to Basic/White Bread and set crust type to Light.

3. Press START.

4. Wait until the cycle completes.

5. Once the loaf is ready, take the bucket out and let the loaf cool for 5 minutes.

6. Gently shake the bucket to remove the loaf.

7. Transfer to a cooling rack, slice, and serve.

**Nutrition**:

- Total Carbs: 23 g

- Fiber: 1 g

- Protein: 5 g

- Fat: 2 g

- Calories: 125

# Crispy French Bread Delight

**Preparation Time**: 10 minutes

**Cooking Time**: 3 – 3 ½ hours

**Servings**: 8

**Ingredients**:

- ⅔ cup water at 80F

- 2 tsp olive oil

- 1 tbsp sugar

- ⅔ tsp salt

- 2 cup white bread flour

- 1 tsp instant yeast

**Directions:**

1. Add all of the ingredients to your bread machine, carefully following the instructions of the manufacturer.

2. Set the program of your bread machine to French Bread and set crust type to Light.

3. Press START.

4. Wait until the cycle completes.

5. Once the loaf is ready, take the bucket out and let the loaf cool for 5 minutes.

6. Gently shake the bucket to remove the loaf.

7. Transfer to a cooling rack, slice, and serve.

**Nutrition:**

- Total Carbs: 26 g
- Fiber: 1 g
- Protein: 3 g
- Fat: 2 g
- Calories: 135

# Chapter 7: Special Bread

## Keto Breakfast Bread

**Preparation Time**: 15 minutes

**Cooking Time**: 40 minutes

**Servings**: 16 slices

**Ingredients**:

- ½ tsp xanthan gum

- ½ tsp salt

- 2 tbsp coconut oil

- ½ cup butter, melted

- 1 tsp baking powder

- 2 cup of almond flour

- 7 eggs

**Directions**:

1. Preheat the oven to 355F.

2. Beat eggs in a bowl on high for 2 minutes.

3. Add coconut oil and butter to the eggs, and continue to beat.

4. Line a loaf pan with baking paper and pour the beaten eggs.

5. Pour in the rest of the ingredients and mix until it becomes thick.

6. Bake until a toothpick comes out dry, about 40 to 45 minutes.

**Nutrition**:

- Calories: 234

- Fat: 23 g

- Carb: 1 g

- Protein: 7 g

# Chia Seed Bread

**Preparation Time**: 10 minutes

**Cooking Time**: 40 minutes

**Servings**: 16 slices

**Ingredients**:

- ½ tsp xanthan gum

- ½ cup butter

- 2 tbsp coconut oil

- 1 tbsp baking powder

- 3 tbsp sesame seeds

- 2 tbsp chia seeds

- ½ tsp salt

- ¼ cup sunflower seeds

- 2 cup almond flour

- 7 eggs

**Directions**:

1. Preheat the oven to 350F.

2. Beat eggs in a bowl on high for 1 to 2 minutes.

3. Beat in the xanthan gum and combine coconut oil and melted butter into eggs, beating continuously.

4. Set aside the sesame seeds, but add the rest of the ingredients.

5. Line a loaf pan with baking paper and place the mixture in it. Top the mixture with sesame seeds.

6. Bake in the oven until a toothpick inserted comes out clean, about 35 to 40 minutes.

**Nutrition**:

- Calories: 405

- Fat: 37 g

- Carb: 4 g

- Protein: 14 g

# Keto Flax Bread

**Preparation Time**: 10 minutes

**Cooking Time**: 18 to 20 minutes

**Servings**: 8

**Ingredients**:

- ¾ cup of water

- 200 g ground flax seeds

- ½ cup psyllium husk powder

- 1 tbsp baking powder

- 7 large egg whites

- 3 tbsp butter

- 2 tsp salt

- ¼ cup granulated stevia

- 1 large whole egg

- 1 ½ cup whey protein isolate

**Directions**:

1. Preheat the oven to 350F.

2. Combine together whey protein isolate, psyllium husk, baking powder, sweetener, and salt.

3. In another bowl, mix together the water, butter, egg, and egg whites.

4. Slowly add psyllium husk mixture to egg mixture and mix well.

5. Lightly grease a bread pan with butter and pour in the batter.

6. Bake in the oven until the bread is set, about 18 to 20 minutes.

**Nutrition:**

- Calories: 265.5

- Fat: 15.68 g

- Carb: 1.88 g

- Protein: 24.34 g

# Special Keto Bread

**Preparation Time**: 15 minutes

**Cooking Time**: 40 minutes

**Servings**: 14

**Ingredients**:

- 2 tsp baking powder
- ½ cup water
- 1 tbsp poppy seeds
- 2 cup fine ground almond meal
- 5 large eggs
- ½ cup olive oil
- ½ tsp fine Himalayan salt

**Directions**:

1. Preheat the oven to 400F.

2. In a bowl, combine salt, almond meal, and baking powder.

3. Drip in oil while mixing until it forms a crumbly dough.

4. Make a little round hole in the middle of the dough and pour eggs into the middle of the dough.

5. Pour water and whisk eggs together with the mixer in the small circle until it is frothy.

6. Start making larger circles to combine the almond meal mixture with the dough until you have a smooth and thick batter.

7. Line your loaf pan with parchment paper.

8. Pour batter into the prepared loaf pan and sprinkle poppy seeds on top.

9. Bake in the oven for 40 minutes on the center rack until firm and golden brown.

10.     Cool in the oven for 30 minutes.

11.     Slice and serve.

**Nutrition**:

- Calories: 227

- Fat: 21 g

- Carb: 4 g

- Protein: 7 g

# Keto Easy Bread

**Preparation Time**: 15 minutes

**Cooking Time**: 45 minutes

**Servings**: 10

**Ingredients**:

- ¼ tsp cream of tartar
- 1 ½ tsp baking powder (double acting)
- 4 large eggs
- 1 ½ cup vanilla whey protein
- ¼ cup olive oil
- ¼ cup coconut milk, unsweetened
- ½ tsp salt
- ¼ cup unsalted butter, softened
- 12 oz cream cheese, softened
- ½ tsp xanthan gum
- ½ tsp baking soda

**Directions**:

1. Preheat oven to 325F.
2. Layer aluminum foil over the loaf pan and spray with olive oil.

3. Beat the butter with cream cheese in a bowl until mixed well.

4. Add oil and coconut milk and blend until mixed. Add eggs one by one until fully mixed. Set aside.

5. In a bowl, whisk whey protein, ½ tsp xanthan gum, baking soda, cream of tartar, salt, and baking powder.

6. Add mixture to egg/cheese mixture and slowly mix until fully combined. Don't over blend.

7. Place in the oven and bake for 40 to 45 minutes, or until golden brown.

8. Cool, slice, and serve.

**Nutrition**:

- Calories: 294.2
- Fat: 24 g
- Carb: 1.8 g
- Protein: 17 g

# Low Carb Bread

**Preparation Time**: 10 minutes

**Cooking Time**: 21 minutes

**Servings**: 12

**Ingredients**:

- 2 cup mozzarella cheese, grated

- 8 oz cream cheese

- Herbs and spices to taste

- 1 tbsp baking powder

- 1 cup crushed pork rinds

- ¼ cup parmesan cheese, grated

- 3 large eggs

**Directions**:

1. Preheat oven to 375F.

2. Line the parchment paper over the baking pan.

3. In a bowl, place cream cheese and mozzarella and microwave for 1 minute on high power. Stir and microwave for 1 minute more. Then stir again.

4. Stir in egg, parmesan, pork rinds, herbs, spices, and baking powder until mixed.

5. Spread mixture on the baking pan and bake until top is lightly brown about 15 to 20 minutes.

6. Cool, slice, and serve.

**Nutrition**:

- Calories: 166

- Fat: 13g

- Carb: 1 g

- Protein: 9 g

# Splendid Low-Carb Bread

**Preparation Time**: 15 minutes

**Cooking Time**: 60 to 70 minutes

**Servings**: 12

**Ingredients**:

- ½ tsp herbs, such as basil, rosemary, or oregano

- ½ tsp garlic or onion powder

- 1 tbsp baking powder

- 5 tbsp psyllium husk powder

- ½ cup almond flour

- ½ cup coconut flour

- ¼ tsp salt

- 1 ½ cup egg whites

- 3 tbsp oil or melted butter

- 2 tbsp apple cider vinegar

- 1/3 to ¾ cup hot water

**Directions**:

1. Grease a loaf pan and preheat the oven to 350F.

2. In a bowl, whisk the salt, psyllium husk powder, onion or garlic powder, coconut flour, almond flour, and baking powder.

3. Stir in egg whites, oil, and apple cider vinegar. Bit by bit, add the hot water, stirring until dough increase in size. Do not add too much water.

4. Mold the dough into a rectangle and transfer to a grease loaf pan.

5. Bake in the oven for 60 to 70 minutes, or until crust feels firm and brown on top.

6. Cool and serve.

**Nutrition**:

- Calories: 97
- Fat: 5.7 g
- Carb: 7.5 g
- Protein: 4.1 g

# Bread De Soul

**Preparation Time**: 10 minutes

**Cooking Time**: 45 minutes

**Servings**: 16

**Ingredients**:

- ¼ tsp cream of tartar

- 2 ½ tsp baking powder

- 1 tsp xanthan gum

- 1/3 tsp baking soda

- ½ tsp salt

- 1 2/3 cup unflavored whey protein

- ¼ cup olive oil

- ¼ cup heavy whipping cream or half and half

- 2 drops of sweet leaf stevia

- 4 eggs

- ¼ cup butter

- 12 oz softened cream cheese

**Directions**:

1. Preheat the oven to 325F.

2. In a bowl, microwave cream cheese and butter for 1 minute.

3. Remove and blend well with a hand mixer.

4. Add olive oil, eggs, heavy cream, and few drops of sweetener and blend well.

5. Blend together the dry ingredients in a separate bowl.

6. Combine the dry ingredients with the wet ingredients and mix with a spoon. Don't use a hand blender to avoid whipping it too much.

7. Grease a bread pan and pour the mixture into the pan.

8. Bake in the oven until golden brown, about 45 minutes.

9. Cool and serve.

**Nutrition**:

- Calories: 200
- Fat: 15.2 g
- Carb: 1.8 g
- Protein: 10 g

# Sandwich Flatbread

**Preparation Time**: 15 minutes

**Cooking Time**: 20 minutes

**Servings**: 10

**Ingredients**:

- ¼ cup water
- ¼ cup oil
- 4 eggs
- ½ tsp salt
- 1/3 cup unflavored whey protein powder
- ½ tsp garlic powder
- 2 tsp baking powder
- 6 tbsp coconut flour
- 3 ¼ cup almond flour

**Directions**:

1. Preheat the oven to 325F.

2. Combine the dry ingredients in a large bowl and mix with a hand whisk.

3. Whisk in eggs, oil, and water until combined well.

4. Place on a piece of large parchment paper and flatten it into a rough rectangle. Place another parchment paper on top.

5. Roll into a large ½ inch to ¾ inch thick rough rectangle. Transfer to the baking sheet and discard the parchment paper on top.

6. Bake until it is firm to the touch, about 20 minutes.

7. Cool and cut into 10 portions.

8. Carefully cut each part into two halves through the bready center. Stuff with your sandwich fillings.

9. Serve.

**Nutrition**:

- Calories: 316

- Fat: 6.8 g

- Carb: 11 g

- Protein: 25.9 g

# Keto Sandwich Bread

**Preparation Time**: 5 minutes

**Cooking Time**: 1 hour

**Servings**: 12

**Ingredients**:

- 1 tsp apple cider vinegar
- ¾ cup water
- ¼ cup avocado oil
- 5 eggs
- ½ tsp salt
- 1 tsp baking soda
- ½ cup coconut flour
- 2 cup plus 2 tbsp almond flour

**Directions**:

1. Preheat the oven to 350F and grease a loaf pan.
2. In a bowl, whisk almond flour, coconut flour, and salt.
3. In another bowl, separate the egg whites from egg yolks. Set egg whites aside.

4. In a blender, blend the oil, egg yolks, water, vinegar, and baking soda for 5 minutes on medium speed until combined.

5. Let the mixture sit for 1 minute, then add in the reserved egg whites and mix until frothy, about 10 to 15 seconds.

6. Add the dry ingredients and process on high for 5 to 10 seconds before the batter becomes too thick for the blender. Blend until the batter is smooth.

7. Transfer batter into the greased loaf pan and smoothen the top.

8. Bake in the oven until a skewer inserted comes out clean, about 50 to 70 minutes.

9. Cool, slice, and serve.

**Nutrition**:

- Calories: 200 g
- Fat: 7 g
- Carb: 7 g
- Protein: 16 g

# Chapter 8: Fruity Bread and Cake

## Banana Bread

**Preparation Time**: 1 hour 40 minutes

**Cooking Time**: 40- 45 minutes

**Servings**: 1 loaf

**Ingredients**:

- 1 tsp baking powder

- 1/2 tsp baking soda

- 2 bananas, peeled and halved lengthwise

- 2 cup all-purpose flour

- 2 eggs

- 3 tbsp vegetable oil

- 3/4 cup white sugar

**Directions**:

1. Put all the ingredients in the bread pan. Select dough setting. Start and mix for about 3-5 minutes.

2. After 3-5 minutes, press stop. Do not continue to mix. Smooth out the top of the dough

3. Using the spatula and then select bake, start and bake for about 50 minutes. After 50 minutes, insert a toothpick into the top center to test doneness.

4. Test the loaf again. When the bread is completely baked, remove the pan from the machine and let the bread remain in the pan for10 minutes. Remove bread and cool in a wire rack.

**Nutrition**:
- Calories: 310
- Total Carbohydrate: 40 g
- Fat: 13 g
- Protein: 3 g

# Blueberry Bread

**Preparation Time**: 3 hours 15 minutes

**Cooking Time**: 40- 45 minutes

**Servings**: 1 loaf

**Ingredients**:

- 1⅛ to 1¼ cup Water
- 6 oz Cream cheese, softened
- 2 tbsp Butter or margarine
- ¼ cup Sugar
- 2 tsp Salt
- 4½ cup Bread flour
- 1½ tsp Grated lemon peel
- 2 tsp Cardamom
- 2 tbsp Nonfat dry milk
- 2½ tsp Red star brand active dry yeast
- ⅔ cup dried blueberries

**Directions**:

1. Place all ingredients except dried blueberries in a bread pan, using the least amount of liquid listed

in the recipe. Select light crust setting and raisin/nut cycle. Press start.

2. Observe the dough as it kneads. After 5 to 10 minutes, if it appears dry and stiff or if your machine sounds as if it's straining to knead it, add more liquid 1 tbsp at a time until dough forms a smooth, soft, pliable ball that is slightly tacky to the touch.

3. At the beep, add the dried blueberries.

4. After the baking cycle ends, remove bread from pan, place on cake rack, and allow to cool 1 hour before slicing.

**Nutrition**:

- Calories: 180

- Total Carbohydrate: 250 g

- Fat: 3 g

- Protein: 9 g

# Apple with Pumpkin Bread

**Preparation Time**: 2 hours 50 minutes

**Cooking Time**: 45 minutes

**Servings**: 2 loaves

**Ingredients**:

- 1/3 cup dried apples, chopped
- 1 1/2 tsp bread machine yeast
- 4 cup bread flour
- 1/3 cup ground pecans
- 1/4 tsp ground nutmeg
- 1/4 tsp ground ginger
- 1/4 tsp allspice
- 1/2 tsp ground cinnamon
- 1 1/4 tsp salt
- 2 tbsp unsalted butter, cubed
- 1/3 cup dry skim milk powder
- 1/4 cup honey
- 2 large eggs, at room temperature
- 2/3 cup pumpkin puree

- 2/3 cup water, with a temperature of 80 to 90 degrees F (26 to 32 degrees C)

**Directions**:

1. Put all ingredients, except the dried apples, in the bread pan in this order: water, pumpkin puree, eggs, honey, skim milk, butter, salt, allspice, cinnamon, pecans, nutmeg, ginger, flour, and yeast.

2. Secure the pan in the machine and lock the lid.

3. Place the dried apples in the fruit and nut dispenser.

4. Turn on the machine. Choose the sweet setting and your desired color of the crust.

5. Carefully unmold the baked bread once done and allow it to cool for 20 minutes before slicing.

**Nutrition**:

- Calories: 228
- Total Carbohydrate: 30 g
- Total Fat: 4 g
- Protein: 18 g

# Chapter 9: Rolls and Pizza

## Cauliflower Pizza Crust

**Preparation Time**: 10 minutes

**Cooking Time**: 35 minutes

**Servings**: 4

**Ingredients**:

- 0.5 tsp salt

- 16 oz Cauliflower florets

- 1 large egg

- 1.5 tbsp coconut flour

- 3 tsp avocado oil

- 0.5 tsp Italian seasoning

- 1 tsp coconut oil

**Directions**:

1. Set your oven to heat at the temperature of 405F.

2. Pulse the cauliflower in a food blender for approximately 60 seconds until it is a crumbly consistency.

3. Heat the coconut oil and cauliflower in a 9"x 9" fry pan for approximately 5 minutes as it becomes tender.

4. Transfer the cauliflower to a kitchen towel and twist to eliminate the extra water. Repeat this step as many times as necessary to make sure the moisture has been eliminated.

5. Prepare your 10" pizza pan or flat sheet with a section of baking lining and set to the side.

6. In a glass dish, blend the riced cauliflower, salt, egg, coconut flour, avocado oil, and Italian seasoning and integrate until it thickens.

7. Flatten the dough onto the prepped pan to no less than a quarter inch.

8. Heat for 25 minutes if thinner then and up to half an hour if thicker.

9. Complete with your favorite toppings and finish on the stove for another 5 minutes. Enjoy!

**Nutrition**:

- Calories: 278

- Fat: 21 g

- Saturated Fat: 2 g

- Protein: 11 g

- Carbohydrates: 5 g

- Sodium: 102 mg

- Fiber: 1 g

- Sugar: 3 g

# Mozzarella Pizza Crust

**Preparation Time**: 7 minutes

**Cooking Time**: 25 minutes

**Servings**: 4

**Ingredients**:

- 1.5 cup mozzarella cheese, shredded

- 0.75 cup almond flour

- 1 whole egg

- 2 tbsp cream cheese, full-Fat

- 0.25 tsp salt

**Directions**:

1. Set your stove to heat at the temperature of 350F.

2. Use a microwave-safe dish to nuke the almond flour, mozzarella, and cream cheese for approximately 60 seconds until liquefied.

3. Toss the cheese and heat for an additional half minute.

4. Blend the salt and egg into the cheese for about half a minute.

5. Place a section of baking lining on the counter and transfer the dough to the middle. Use another section of baking lining to place on top.

6. Flatten to no less than a quarter of an inch. Separate the top baking lining and transfer to 10" pan.

7. Heat for approximately 13 minutes until turning golden.

8. Layer with your toppings of choice and heat for about 5 minutes.

9. Serve hot and enjoy!

**Nutrition**:

- Calories: 190

- Carbohydrates: 1.4 g

- Fat: 6 g

- Saturated Fat: 1 g

- Fiber: 2 g

- Sugar: 2 g

# Zucchini Pizza Crust

**Preparation Time**: 15 minutes

**Cooking Time**: 45 minutes

**Servings**: 4

**Ingredients**:

- 4 cup zucchini, shredded

- 1 cup almond flour

- 2.75 tbsp coconut flour

- 4 tbsp Nutritional yeast

- 1.33 tbsp Italian seasoning

- 0.75 tsp salt

- 3 large eggs

**Directions**:

1. Adjust the temperature of your stove to heat at 400F.

2. Cover a 12.75" pan with a layer of baking lining and set to the side.

3. Use a kitchen grater to shred the zucchini using the largest holes available.

4. Transfer to a kitchen towel and wring to release all excess moisture.

5. In a glass dish, blend the coconut flour, zucchini, salt, Italian seasoning, Nutritional yeast, eggs, and almond flour until integrated and thickened.

6. Distribute to the prepped sheet and flatten to no less than quarter an inch by hand.

7. Heat for the duration of 20 minutes, and then turn the crust over and warm for another 10 minutes.

8. Layer the pizza with your preferred toppings and heat for another 13 minutes.

9. Wait about 10 minutes before slicing and serving. Enjoy!

**Nutrition**:

- Calories: 127

- Protein: 7 g

- Fat: 8 g

- Saturated Fat: 2 g

- Carbohydrates: 4 g

- Fiber: 1 g

- Sugar: 2 g

# Fat Head Pizza Dough - Egg & Gluten-Free

**Preparation Time**: 15 minutes

**Cooking Time**: 30minutes

**Servings**: 8

**Ingredients**:

- 8 oz Mozzarella cheese slices full Fat

- 2 tbsp grated parmesan cheese

- 2 tbsp full-Fat cream cheese

- 1/3 cup almond flour

- ½ tsp garlic powder

- ½ tsp salt

- 2 tbsp whole psyllium husks, either whole or ground

**Directions**:

1. Finely chop and place the mozzarella in a microwaveable container. Cook until melted. (this took about 1.5 minutes.)

2. Let the cheese cool slightly. Mix with the cream cheese, almond flour, parmesan cheese, garlic powder, and salt. (knead in with your hands.) Add the psyllium and shape the dough into a ball and then roll out as flat as you can on parchment paper, pizza stone, or a silicone mat.

3. Shape the dough as needed and bake at 425F for about 15-20 minutes.

4. Flip the crust and bake for about 5 more minutes until browned.

5. Add the sauce, cheese, and other toppings. Bake for about five more minutes.

**Nutrition**:

- Calories: 161
- Fat: 13 g
- Saturated Fat: 1 g
- Carbohydrates: 2 g

- Protein: 9 g

- Sodium: 132 mg

- Fiber: 0 g

- Sugar: 2 g

# Keto Pizza Pockets

**Preparation Time**: 5 minutes

**Cooking Time**: 7 minutes

**Servings**:4

**Ingredients**:

- 1 ¾ cup pre-shredded/grated cheese mozzarella

- ¾ cup almond flour

- 2 tbsp full-Fat cream cheese

- 1 medium egg

- 1 pinch salt

**Directions**:

1. Mix the shredded cheese, cream cheese, and almond flour in a microwaveable bowl. Microwave using high power for one minute.

2. Stir and continue cooking on high for another 30 seconds.

3. Whisk the egg and salt and mix gently with the rest of the fixings.

4. Roll the dough between two sheets of parchment baking paper. (Don't roll as thin as a thin pizza crust so it can hold the chosen fillings.) Discard the

top baking paper. Slice the dough into squares (the same size as your toasted sandwich maker).

5. Place one square on the bottom of the sandwich maker; add your choice of fillings.

6. Place another square of dough on the top and press the lid of the sandwich maker down.

7. Cook until they're golden brown or about three to five minutes.

**Nutrition**:

- Calories: 293

- Fat: 3.9 g

- Saturated Fat: 2 g

- Protein: 15.6 g

- Carbohydrates: 1.8 g

- Sodium: 96 mg

- Fiber: 0 g

- Sugar: 1 g

# Conclusion

Bread is considered as the basic necessity for survival in life. Everyone consumes the bread according to his or her own choices and preferences. It is also observed that bread is preferred over any other food item. Variation in the bread-making occurs from country to country as well. The key ingredients in bread making are flour, yeast, oil, water, salt, sugar, milk, and eggs. Each of them imparts different and unique characteristics of the bread. Even the quantity of these key ingredients can largely affect the end product. Over the past few years, advancement in technology has made home chores easier, making kitchen work easier to handle. One such innovation is that of a bread maker.

A bread maker or bread machine is a home-made bread making appliance. Bread has also been consumed along with all sorts of food, thereby making it essential in all meals, whether it be breakfast, lunch, or dinner. While the results of baking may vary considerably from one bread machine to the other, the flavor of bread baked in a device is opposite from that of bread baked in the oven, even if the same recipe is used. Besides, bread maker bread has a heavier and more dense consistency rather than lightweight and airy.

Bread machines are getting popular day by day due to their level of convenience in use. Taking into consideration the convenience of using bread machines, it is suggested that they are user friendly, which means that it can be dealt with great ease. It also gives the user opportunity to experiment and explore different ingredients and types of bread in the comfort of their own home. It provides the consumer with freshly baked bread whenever needed.

CPSIA information can be obtained
at www.ICGtesting.com
Printed in the USA
BVHW051028210721
612519BV00002B/150